THE 100% **OFFICIAL**

PIGGY™

SURVIVAL MANUAL

ISBN 978-1-338-86465-6

10 9 8 7 6 5 4 3 2   23 24 25 26 27

Printed in the U.S.A.   40

First printing 2023

Book interior designed, written, and packaged by Dynamo Limited.

THE 100% OFFICIAL

PIGGY™

SURVIVAL MANUAL

SCHOLASTIC INC.

CONTENTS

THE STRANGE AND TERRIFYING WORLD OF PIGGY

PIGGY is one of the biggest indie games of the last five years, with over eleven billion visits! It's a survival horror game set in Lucella, a city of colorful cartoon animals, which has been struck by a mysterious infection that causes uncontrollable rage.

The player must investigate this grim situation—and survive. Unfortunately, every place you visit along the way is a puzzle to get out of.

In this book we'll profile the characters who populate the world of *PIGGY* and take you through its story, chapter by chapter. If you're worried it might not be safe, let us set your mind at rest: It definitely isn't . . .

GOING SOLO

If you want to experience the story of Piggy chapter by chapter, set up a private server that you can play solo or with like-minded friends. This way you'll get your own choice of map and can make all the discoveries for yourself!

CHAPTER 1—HOUSE

ANTAGONIST: Piggy

NOTES: 0

It all starts outside a large family home. A police officer (the player) has driven up looking for a missing child. They get out of their car . . . and are immediately hit over the head.

They wake up inside the house and realize they've been kidnapped—and must escape

MISSING PERSONS
REPORT

DESCRIPTION:
Young Pig, male, dressed in blue. Ran away from home and not seen since. Possible sighting on way to city?

while avoiding their kidnapper, Piggy. However, many of the doors are locked—and the front door is boarded up. This house is home to a family of pigs—but there's no one to be seen other than Piggy . . .

Once the officer escapes from the house, they return to the police station to seek help.

TIPS

The house has five stories, including an attic, a basement, and an underground garage. Start by looking for the green key. The wrench is necessary to get past the laser gate. Completing the gear box activates the well, bringing up the white key that will open the front door—though you also need the code and the hammer.

CHAPTER 2—STATION

ANTAGONIST: Mother

NOTES: 4

The officer finds the police station deserted. The voice of their colleague, Doggy, comes over a loudspeaker: "Attention! A monster is in the station! Get to the garage now!"

The "monster" is another Pig, who is stalking the station and attacking anyone who comes near. If the officer didn't realize

TIPS

The station has two levels. There's an acid river running across one of the rooms—NPCs can cross this, so don't think you're safe on the other side! This is the first chapter to have notes scattered across it, which provide clues to the game's lore. The ultimate aim is to reach the garage, where Doggy has barricaded himself—he has a car, but a can of gasoline is necessary to complete the escape.

FROM Chief

TO All Recipients

SUB URGENT

Can someone please explain why ALL the cells are empty? Who released the prisoners?!

things were seriously wrong before, they do now . . .

Once they get out, Doggy and the officer share experiences.

"Man, we seriously need to find out what's going on," Doggy remarks.

"I know," the officer replies. "I've started to see these things all over the place."

Figuring it all out will call on their detective skills—but they've got a more immediate problem, because the car's gas is already running out . . .

CHAPTER 3—GALLERY

With the car out of gas, Doggy and the officer are trapped in the middle of the city and surrounded by infected citizens. The only place they can reach is the gallery, where they investigated a robbery a month earlier. They run and take cover there—but one of the Infected has gotten in, too . . .

IMPORTANT NOTICE

The gallery will be closing early today due to staff illness. Please do not touch anyone on your way out.

Once the officer and Doggy escape, they realize the Infected can't be stopped and they certainly can't be arrested. After a little pep talk from Doggy, they decide to leave the city . . .

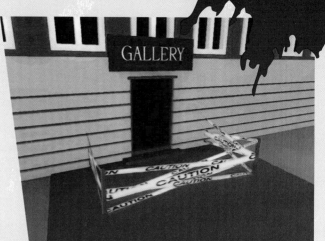

TIPS

The gallery is spread across three levels. The spiral staircase is difficult to take quickly without falling off, and there are also several small rooms where it's easy to get cornered. In this chapter, the player has an NPC who helps them for the first time: if you give Doggy a bone, he will stun the antagonist for you. The bones can be found in the yellow safe (on the second floor) or the purple safe (on the third floor).

CHAPTER 4—FOREST

ANTAGONIST: Sheepy

NOTES: 0

The officer and Doggy have been hiding out in the forest for four weeks, wondering what has happened to their friends in the city and surviving by traveling to small towns and taking supplies. One night, the officer is awoken by a barking noise—and realizes Doggy has gone.

ACTIVITIES

Tonight the whole campsite is invited to play a game of tag. Hide where you can—the last one to avoid getting tagged is the winner!

Doggy has been infected by someone unknown—and Sheepy, who they previously encountered at the gallery, has also found her way to the forest. The officer no longer has any friends out there . . . Outside the walls of the campsite, the officer finds a dropped walkie-talkie. A voice comes from it: "Hello? Is anyone out there?"

TIPS

The infected Doggy doesn't attack, but if he finds you, he will bark and alert Sheepy to your location. As with the gallery, this chapter has a tricky climbing element—the tree house, which must be accessed by walking up a series of narrow planks.

CHAPTER 5—SCHOOL

The voice on the other end of the walkie-talkie is Mr. P, a billionaire and well-liked public figure. He wants the officer to rescue his friend who is trapped in the school. An infected teacher is

I will not go near the Infected
I will not go near the Infected
I will not go near the Infected
I will not go near the Infected
I will not go near the Infected
I will not go near the Infected
I will not go near t

stalking the corridors, and she seems to have forgotten you're not allowed to hit kids with your ruler these days.

After escaping the school, the officer meets Mr. P in the sewers as instructed, with a sense of surprise at encountering the island's richest inhabitant in such a place. However, the officer then passes out and is rushed to the hospital. The last thing they see before falling unconscious again is a hallucination of Doggy . . .

TIPS

Bunny is hiding in a surveillance room. Once you find her, she becomes an ally and will temporarily knock out the teacher if given carrots. As with the bones in the gallery, these can be found in the yellow or purple safes.

CHAPTER 6—HOSPITAL

The officer wakes up to learn they've received treatment and they seem to be pulling through, despite being exposed to the Infection: They haven't developed full-blown symptoms. That's the good news. The bad news is that the hospital is being evacuated because one of the doctors, Beary, has become infected.

TIPS

Bunny remains with you as an ally, and as before, she can be given a carrot to stun Beary temporarily. There's just one carrot here, in the yellow safe. This chapter also features the first appearance of vials, which need to be filled in order to work.

Your aim is to make your way to the helipad on the roof, where Mr. P is supposed to be waiting for you with a helicopter—but when you get there, he has left without you. (This happens no matter how quickly you complete the chapter. Rude!)

MEDICAL CHART

Patient appears unresponsive. Little sign of infection but perhaps the patient has some other weakness that means their body cannot cope with Substance 128 at all. Suggest discontinuing treatment.

No—we will not give up! Treatment will continue.

CHAPTER 7—METRO

NOTES: 3

The officer seeks another way out of the hospital, going to the Metro station located directly beneath it. The train isn't working, so the officer must fix it. Bunny takes a rest on the platform by the train—she doesn't quite seem to be feeling right. And a hideous zombielike creature is chasing you . . .

PLEASE BE POLITE TO OUR STAFF

Aggressive incidents on the Metro network are on the rise. There's no excuse. We reserve the right to refuse entry!

After the train is repaired, Bunny confesses she was given a bottle of some potion by Mr. P, which she drank. "I didn't know it would soon turn me into . . ." she says before trailing off. Knowing she is about to become one of the Infected, she tells the officer to leave her behind—she'll hold off the other Infected as long as she can.

TIPS

Metro has one of the game's simpler layouts: Apart from the platform there's a waiting room and another room beyond a barrier. Below is a maintenance level, with three staircases connecting it to the upper level, which should help you avoid getting cornered. Two coins are needed to operate the vending machine and get the blue keycard.

CHAPTER 8—CARNIVAL

ANTAGONISTS: Clowny and Foxy

NOTES: 4

The officer rides the Metro to the site of a carnival owned by Mr. P, hoping to find him there. It's become clear now that he's responsible for the infection via the medicine he's been giving out. However, the place seems deserted, except for Clowny . . .

TIPS

This map is not large and is pretty open, making it easier to find your way around. The plank needs to be placed at the top of the steps in the main circus tent, while the water gun needs to be used at one of the stalls. Watch out for the hall of mirrors, which at first glance seems to be empty but contains a safe!

Performing today at 8:00 p.m.

CLOWNY

His laughter is infectious! Everyone can get involved! Surprises guaranteed!

Along the way, the officer must open a cage in order to obtain a white key—and in doing so releases another Infected. In the building that leads out of the carnival, the officer finds two uninfected citizens, who realize the officer can't be infected because "the Infected don't talk." They save the officer from the Infected who has been released—and offer to take them to a safe location.

CHAPTER 9—CITY

ANTAGONISTS: Elly and Grandmother

NOTES: 4

The Safe Place is in the city—they can see it from the roof of one of the buildings. However, the officer and their new friends discover the gate leading to it is locked and on fire, so they must find a way to extinguish the fire and open the gate.

TODAY'S SPECIAL

Poutine with Grandma's Mystery Special Sauce!

Watch out—it's got a KICK to it!

The buildings here include a hotel, the headquarters of Elly Enterprises, and a shop called Grandma Piggy's Poutine. The owners of the last two have both become infected and are roaming the streets.

Once the gate is open, the officer tells their story:

That what began as a search for a missing child has led to the discovery that Mr. P has been causing the Infection with his potions. He has to be stopped. Then they hear a strange noise coming from a dumpster . . .

TIPS

In previous chapters, the carrot is an optional item used to make the NPC stun the antagonist. Here it's different: You must feed your ally the carrot to make him break the planks across the code input system. Also note you'll need the fire extinguisher twice—to put out the fire at the gate, and also the one on the roof of Elly Enterprises.

CHAPTER 10—MALL

ANTAGONISTS: Robby and Mousy

NOTES: 6

The officer goes toward the source of the noise, and follows a mysterious figure. They end up at a mall, where they encounter a noninfected adversary in the form of Robby, a security droid who has been upgraded to keep out any intruders . . .

TIPS

The mall has two levels. The secondary antagonist, Mousy, is confined to the vent—you don't need to go far into the vent to use the wrench, so avoiding Mousy isn't difficult. You have an ally who can be fed grass to make her stun Robby—grass can be found in the bank vault, near the upstairs vending machines, or in Kitty's Kitchen.

HOW TO USE YOUR
MALL ROBOT

The security level on your robot can be adjusted to suit your needs. Call our sales team if you wish to purchase the Chainsaw Arm accessory, which is simple to fit and is guaranteed to deter any intruder—or your money back!

Somewhere in a storage room, the person they followed there is hiding—Georgie, who the officer has been looking for all this time. He explains that after his family started acting weird, he went to the city to find his grandmother (who the officer has met near her poutine shop).

Back at The Safe Place, the survivors have traced Mr. P's helicopter. The officer heads off to confront him . . .

CHAPTER 11—OUTPOST

ANTAGONISTS: Torcher and Soldiers

NOTES: 6

The helicopter the officer is following lands at a military outpost. The Soldiers at the outpost are infected: The only other person there is Torcher, who carries a flamethrower and whose true identity is hidden behind a mask.

* * * NEW ORDERS * * *

We have a code 19 situation. Infection in city. All leave is canceled. All Soldiers to your posts. If your comrade shows signs of infection, report it immediately!

When the officer and his companions reach the plant within the outpost, they discover Georgie has followed them, despite being told to stay at The Safe Place—and several of the Soldiers have followed him. Georgie wants to see the person responsible for hurting his family, so the officer takes him into the plant while the others hold off the Soldiers.

Mr. P is inside, but he's turned himself into a cyborg and seems to be losing his grip on reality. He thinks the officer and Georgie are dead, and tells them so, then he runs away . . .

TIPS

This chapter works differently from others—it has multiple Soldiers, who appear from holes in the ground. Your ally follows you and attacks them, causing them to vanish. The tank needs to be fueled and then equipped with a missile to blow open one of the doors.

DISTORTED MEMORY

ANTAGONIST: Memory

NOTES: 4

This extra chapter takes place from Georgie's point of view. At the start he seems to be waking from a nightmare, but it quickly becomes clear this is the nightmare. He's inside a strange and distorted version of his own home, pursued by a nightmarish version of his mother.

TIPS

This was initially available for only a limited time before the release of Chapter 12. It remains unavailable on public servers but can now be accessed on VIP servers. Though it's based on the map from Chapter 1, the layout is very different, with holes in the walls revealing new areas. The dinosaur and robot toys must be placed on the toy altar to get the white key.

The dream is the same every time—I wake up in my house, but it's not my house. All I can do is get out. Sometimes I make it. Sometimes I don't . . .

Notes on the walls describe what happened: His family volunteered to test the cure and left him on his own. They seemed fine when they came back but then started to change. "Now you relive that night every time you sleep." Once Georgie escapes the dream house, he feels the Infection starting to grip him—and then wakes up in his hiding place at the mall . . .

CHAPTER 12—PLANT

The officer and Georgie catch up with Mr. P, who tells them he just wants to be alone. He still believes they're memories tormenting him, and has every intention of stopping them. He readies his gun arm . . .

Can the Infection be cured? Looking for cures caused this in the first place. I give up . . . I'll just stay here, away from everyone else. Perhaps it will all blow over . . .

After surviving events at the plant, including an explosion that brings in parts of previous chapters, the officer and Georgie force Mr. P to reconsider his actions. The officer prevents Georgie from hurting Mr. P, telling Georgie this would only turn him into the very thing he hates.

Mr. P tells the officer he'll go on fighting the Infected while they escape . . . and the officer has a choice. Stay with Mr. P, or escape with Georgie?

TIPS

There are three endings. The Good Ending sees you escape with Georgie. The Bad Ending involves staying with Mr. P and getting infected by Badgy. If you have obtained both endings and all other badges, you can get the True Ending. For this you must also play a round of Player + Bot mode on Chapter 9, open the exit, then find a picture of Mrs. P under a purple car and leave while holding it. Then play through the plant again and choose to stay with Mr. P at the end.

THE TRUTH . . .

When Mr. P's wife, Mrs. P, developed the very rare Linnaeoma disease, he devoted himself to finding a cure. He donated 40 percent of his fortune to research facilities across the nation.

LINNAEOMA DISEASE

WHAT IS IT?

Not much is known about the disease. Doctors are still researching it—there have been very few cases so far. It seems to be restricted to Lucella—so if you catch it, please don't travel!

Mr. P formed a team of researchers to seek a cure for the disease. He believed he'd found it in the form of something called Substance 128. He was warned by doctors that Substance 128 was unstable, but still sought volunteers to test it on.

WHAT HAPPENS WHEN YOU CATCH IT?

Again, research is still in the early stages. But the disease has a huge impact on the lives of its sufferers.

HOW CAN I HELP?

If you're a sufferer of Linnaeoma disease, please get in touch with Mr. P's research foundation. The more we know, the closer we get to a cure!

MEDICAL RECORDS

Three members of a family of pigs agreed to act as test subjects for Substance 128. They reported positive results at first, and Mr. P took this to mean it worked. He rushed to give the cure to Mrs. P . . .

OBSERVATION NOTES

• No negative reaction from the test subjects after being given Substance 128. The medicine seems to be safe.

• Shortly after their dose, all three subjects reported feeling energized and stronger.

• Results suggest that even if Substance 128 is not a complete cure for Linnaeoma, it should help sufferers by easing their symptoms. It may give them strength to fight the disease.

• Subjects should be monitored, just in case of unforeseen side effects, but can leave the hospital.

However, after the family returned home they started to become more aggressive and their eyes turned red. Substance 128 wasn't a cure at all: It was an Infection, turning everyone who came into contact with it into zombielike beings gripped by an uncontrollable rage. The youngest member of the family fled the house.

Mrs. P was showing the same changes as the family. Mr. P couldn't bring himself to stop her, so he let her go—and decided to fund research into curing the virus instead . . .

PIGGY/PENNY PIGGY

FIRST STORY APPEARANCE: Book 1, Chapter 1
SKIN INTRODUCED: Book 1, Chapter 1
OBTAINABLE: Default Skin
WEAPON: Baseball Bat

Piggy, once known as Penny Piggy, was one of the original volunteer test subjects for Substance 128, along with her parents. This is how she became infected. Only her younger brother, who hadn't taken the experimental medicine, avoided infection.

Piggy also appears in a distorted form. This version is larger but also affected by a dark substance that seems to have eaten away at the left side of her body. She can be obtained as a playable skin by collecting all the pages of the Player's Journal in Book 1.

 DOGGY

FIRST STORY APPEARANCE: Book 1, Chapter 2
SKIN INTRODUCED: Book 1, Chapter 2
OBTAINABLE: 275 Tokens
WEAPON: Firefighter's Axe

Doggy is one of the game's major characters. Before the Infection he worked at the Lucella Police Department and was the player's partner and friend. In Chapter 2, Station, Doggy gives you important information over the intercom and the chapter can be completed by finding him in the garage and refueling his car.

After you leave with Doggy he continues to help you at the gallery, but in the forest he becomes infected and the player must leave him there. He reappears in Book 2 in flashbacks and hallucinations.

 # SHEEPY

FIRST STORY APPEARANCE: Book 1, Chapter 3
SKIN INTRODUCED: Book 1, Chapter 1
OBTAINABLE: 150 tokens
WEAPON: Sledgehammer

Sheepy is first encountered by the player in Chapter 3, where she (along with Mother and Father) surround Doggy's car. After escaping the car, the player must hide in the gallery. In the following chapter Sheepy appears again, this time in the forest alongside the infected Doggy.

A note in the laboratory in Chapter 12 mentions Sheepy: "Mrs. P, Sheepy, Bunny . . . Our initial group is gone. Now the researchers are, too. I am truly alone." This suggests Sheepy was one of those researchers working on the cure for Linnaeoma disease.

ANGEL

SKIN INTRODUCED: Book 1, Chapter 4
FIRST STORY APPEARANCE: N/A
OBTAINABLE: 250 Tokens
WEAPON: Rod of Asclepius

This skin is, obviously, an angelic version of Piggy with wings and a halo. Her weapon comes from Greek mythology—Asclepius, the god of healing, carried a rod with a snake curled around it. The model for the rod (listed as Staff of the Winds) can be found in the game catalog, as can Angel's wings (listed as Sparkling Angel Wings).

A redesigned version of Angel with more elaborate robes and a jewel-topped staff appears in *PIGGY: Hunt*, the Steam edition of the game.

🐻 TEACHER

FIRST STORY APPEARANCE: Book 1, Chapter 5
SKIN INTRODUCED: Book 1, Chapter 3
OBTAINABLE: 175 Tokens
WEAPON: Ruler

The Teacher is a gazelle. Prior to the Infection, she taught at the school, but after becoming infected by Substance 128, she wanders the school's corridors attacking those who enter.

The Teacher is the main antagonist of Chapter 5 and chases you while you try to locate Bunny and escape with her into the sewers. The Teacher is left behind in the school when the chapter is completed. She can be seen in the credits of both books, and in Book 2 she is cured and teaching at the school again.

SKELLY

FIRST STORY APPEARANCE: Book 1, Chapter 5
SKIN INTRODUCED: Book 1, Chapter 6
OBTAINABLE: 375 Tokens
WEAPON: None

Skelly first appeared as an educational prop in the science room of the school, and wasn't supposed to be a character or a skin. However, due to demand from players, Skelly was introduced as a skin along with the next chapter. Skelly carries no weapon—or anything else—and so attacks using their hands.

Skelly also featured in Book 2 as part of the limited Spooky Hunt event: By collecting parts in alleys, Skelly could be reconstructed, thereby earning the Tombstone Trap. However, this event has since finished.

 BEARY

FIRST STORY APPEARANCE: Book 1, Chapter 6
SKIN INTRODUCED: Book 1, Chapter 6
OBTAINABLE: 290 Tokens
WEAPON: Falchion

Beary is an antagonist in Chapter 6, Hospital. He was formerly a doctor at the hospital and may have been one of those seeking a cure for Linnaeoma disease. However, he later became infected when the hospital was raided: He's the doctor mentioned in the Player's Journal who became infected and triggered a panic.

Beary's weapon, the falchion, is a type of one-handed sword used in Europe between the thirteenth and sixteenth centuries. These are not commonly found in hospitals.

CLOWNY

FIRST STORY APPEARANCE: Book 1, Chapter 8
SKIN INTRODUCED: Book 1, Chapter 8
OBTAINABLE: 385 Tokens
WEAPON: Comedy Mallet

It's hard to tell what kind of animal Clowny is under that makeup, and we don't want to get close enough to find out. He was formerly a clown at the carnival, but when the Infection spread, he started to roam the site attacking others.

Clowny is noted for having one of the most elaborate jumpscares of any character in the game—he spins his whole body 360 degrees while hitting you with his mallet and hooting with laughter.

🐘 ELLY

FIRST STORY APPEARANCE: Book 1, Chapter 9
SKIN INTRODUCED: Book 1, Chapter 9
OBTAINABLE: 310 Tokens
WEAPON: Polearm

Elly is an Elephant and businessperson. She runs a company called Elly Enterprises—or at least she did before getting infected. She first appears in Chapter 9, City, where she can be found roaming the city with Grandmother. Not that you *want* to find her . . .

Elly makes a further appearance at the end of Book 1, where she's part of the infected army that's summoned to the Doveport military camp and battles Sergeant Monroe's faction. Her weapon can be found in the game catalog as Tribal Spear.

🐷 DEVIL

FIRST STORY APPEARANCE: N/A
SKIN INTRODUCED: With Traitor Gamemode
OBTAINABLE: 270 Tokens
WEAPON: Trident

This counterpart to the Angel skin depicts a devilish version of Piggy, with horns and red wings. Again, the wings and weapon are in the game catalog as Crimson Wings and Trident—though the trident has been recolored for use in *PIGGY*. Like Angel, Devil hovers just above the ground instead of walking on it.

Devil was introduced along with Giraffy and the Traitor gamemode, celebrating one billion visits on game, in April 2020.
The *PIGGY: Hunt* version adds flames above Devil's head and on the trident.

🐽 GIRAFFY

FIRST STORY APPEARANCE: Book 1, Chapter 10
SKIN INTRODUCED: With Traitor Gamemode
OBTAINABLE: 285 Tokens
WEAPON: Club

Like Devil, Giraffy was introduced at the same time as Traitor gamemode, but unlike Devil, he has a story role, too. He's a former biology student and counselor at the forest camp, and he's briefly seen in Book 1. There, he appears as one of the survivors rescued and brought to The Safe Place.

Giraffy appears much more in Book 2, where he's part of the group at The Safe Place: In Chapter 4, he's been locked in his room and must be released by the player. After being shot by Willow in Chapter 5, Sewers, Giraffy needs to be looked after and he's not seen after Chapter 6 until the end of the Savior branch.

MIMI

FIRST STORY APPEARANCE: Book 1, Chapter 10
SKIN INTRODUCED: Book 1, Chapter 10
OBTAINABLE: 235 Tokens
WEAPON: Pickaxe

Mimi is a Mole, hence she carries a pickaxe for digging. The NPC version of Mimi appears briefly in Book 1, but has a far more substantial role in Book 2: She's one of The Safe Place group of survivors and can be found in Chapter 1. She's an ally to the player throughout the first half of the game.

In Chapter 7, Factory, things get interesting—if you get the Survivor Ending of this chapter, Mimi stays behind to help Giraffy and the members of The Silver Paw. If you get the Savior Ending, Mimi comes with you and remains with you until the end of the game.

 ROBBY

FIRST STORY APPEARANCE: Book 1, Chapter 10
SKIN INTRODUCED: Book 1, Chapter 10
OBTAINABLE: 475 Tokens
WEAPON: Chainsaw Arm

There are two Robbys, both robot pigs with a similar design—but they're different characters with different roles in the story. The first Robby, encountered in Book 1 at the mall, is a security droid that seems to have gone rogue. This version can also be acquired as a skin.

Another Robby appears in Book 2 and is purely an NPC. This Robby enters the story in Chapter 9, Docks, and is an ally: It was built as another mall security robot, but due to a malfunction it was repurposed as Kona's assistant.

MOUSY

FIRST STORY APPEARANCE: Book 1, Chapter 10
SKIN INTRODUCED: With Build Mode
OBTAINABLE: 415 Tokens
WEAPON: Half Nunchuck

Mousy is a secondary antagonist at the mall, where she crawls around the vent in a circuit, preventing the player from hiding in the vent to avoid Robby. You must also go into the vent to use the wrench and access the room where the green keycard is.

The NPC of Mousy doesn't carry a weapon, but the skin version comes with a broken nunchuck. Another significant difference is that the skin has legs! The NPC doesn't, which maybe explains the crawling.

 TORCHER

FIRST STORY APPEARANCE: Book 1, Chapter 11
SKIN INTRODUCED: Book 1, Chapter 11
OBTAINABLE: 550 Tokens
WEAPON: Flamethrower

Torcher can be found at the outpost. It's unclear just what he is, because he wears a gas mask at all times. He's part of the military operation, and may or may not be infected—however, this doesn't make much difference to the player. Even if he's not infected, he's lost control of the situation and will attack you regardless.

Torcher will use his flamethrower on you as his jumpscare, engulfing you in flame. Somewhere in the outpost there's an encrypted message you can decode: This may have been written by Torcher.

SOLDIER

FIRST STORY APPEARANCE: Book 1, Chapter 11
SKIN INTRODUCED: Book 1, Chapter 11
OBTAINABLE: 315 Tokens
WEAPON: Combat Knife

The Soldier isn't just one character—there are several of them in the outpost in Chapter 11. However, they're all pigs and they all have the same dark scar on the side of their face. (The version in *PIGGY: Hunt* has a redder scar, indicating the injury was a severe burn.)

The Soldiers are infected, and though they don't chase the player, you still have to avoid them—coming into contact with them means death. The Soldier also appears in some endings of Book 1.

BADGY

FIRST STORY APPEARANCE: Book 1, Chapter 12
SKIN INTRODUCED: Book 1, Chapter 12
OBTAINABLE: 335 Tokens
WEAPON: Vial

The player encounters Badgy at Plant, the final chapter of Book 1—and all the evidence suggests he was formerly a member of the research team into Linnaeoma disease, and was infected while looking for the cure.

A note found at the plant, possibly written by Badgy, suggests he came into direct contact with Substance 128 while moving their equipment. Is that Substance 128 in that vial he carries—which seems to have turned his arm bright green? We don't want to find out . . .

 MEMORY

FIRST STORY APPEARANCE: Book 1, Distorted Memory
SKIN INTRODUCED: Book 1, Chapter 2
OBTAINABLE: 200 Tokens
WEAPON: Black Baseball Bat

Memory resembles Piggy's mother but with a monochrome appearance. She's the antagonist of Distorted Memory, which suggests she herself is a distorted version of Mother. Notably, she also levitates slightly above the ground. She pursues Georgie through the distorted house.

A variant of Memory known as Glitchy was introduced as part of an event tying into the release of the book *Ready Player Two*, and is found in a secret location called Maple Donut's Hideout in Book 2, Chapter 1. This version is black with glowing eyes, one blue and one green, and is the primary bot in this area.

PARASEE

FIRST STORY APPEARANCE: N/A
SKIN INTRODUCED: Book 1, Distorted Memory
OBTAINABLE: 425 Tokens
WEAPON: None

Parasee is a Pig . . . with tentacles. Which just seems unnecessary. Their name comes from the fact they're a parasite version of Piggy. The tentacles can be found in the game catalog—they're listed as Tentacled Alien Left Arm and Tentacled Alien Right Arm. Instead of a weapon, Parasee attacks with their tentacles.

Parasee doesn't appear in the story—they were designed to be part of Distorted Memory but ultimately didn't feature in the chapter when it was released, with their role taken by Memory.

GHOSTY

FIRST STORY APPEARANCE: N/A
SKIN INTRODUCED: 2020 Custom Skin Contest
OBTAINABLE: 460 Tokens
WEAPON: Cutlass

Ghosty was the runner-up in the 2020 Custom Skin Contest, designed by Centcrisped. They are a ghost pirate Bear with hat, eye patch, and cutlass . . . and no legs, or a left hand.

At least, they don't have legs or a left hand we can *see*. What remains of their body is semitransparent, and when Ghosty moves we can hear footsteps—which strongly suggests they *do* have legs, we just can't see them. At least being a ghost means you can't be infected by Substance 128, right . . . ? Oh.

TEN SIGNS YOU'RE A PIGGY ADDICT

 You put locks on every room in your house, with color-coded keys.

You avoid anyone with pinkeye.

 When you arrive anywhere new, you like to find out if you'll need a plank and where it is.

You read all the notes on other people's refrigerators in case they contain any clues to the lore.

 You find yourself looking for glitches that help you walk to school faster.

You ask your friends for help by offering them a carrot.

 When people enter a room you're in, you run around a table and out through the door.

 You refer to your bedroom as your "spawn point."

 You don't entirely trust wolves.

 You never, ever, ever stop moving if you can help it.

CHAPTER 1—ALLEYS

ANTAGONIST: Rash

NOTES: 4

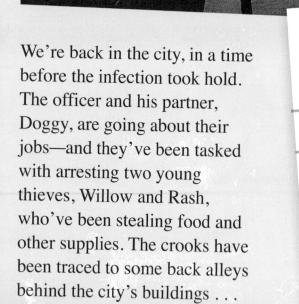

We're back in the city, in a time before the infection took hold. The officer and his partner, Doggy, are going about their jobs—and they've been tasked with arresting two young thieves, Willow and Rash, who've been stealing food and other supplies. The crooks have been traced to some back alleys behind the city's buildings . . .

FOOD THIEVES TERRORIZE CITY!

"No Meal Is Safe," Police Warn

Lucella has been rocked by a series of robberies involving food. Panicking citizens are being advised to keep their kitchens locked and not leave groceries unattended, even for a short period.

The Infection plays no part in this chapter—instead, the officer is searching for Willow while Rash tries to stop them. After Willow is caught, she pleads she was just trying to feed her family. The officer wonders if arresting them is the right thing to do—while Doggy says they're just doing what they have to. After this, we return to the post-infection world and The Safe Place, continuing on from the events of Book 1. Mimi wants to get a radio working, but for that they need to get batteries from the Store . . .

TIPS

Doggy is an ally in this chapter and can be given batteries to knock out Rash. You need a three-digit code for the final stage, which changes every time—find the digits in the back room of Daisy's TVs, inside the room that needs to be opened with the screwdriver, and at the end of the hallway where the water spill is. If you get two numbers, you can try going through all other options for the third.

CHAPTER 2—STORE

ANTAGONIST: Dessa

NOTES: 4

The officer goes to the Store with two friends, aiming to grab the batteries and then leave immediately. However the errand is complicated by an infected former employee of the Store, Dessa, who's chasing down anyone who enters.

TIPS

This is a major chapter in terms of story, but the chapter itself is quite straightforward. Dessa will spawn in the metro in the parking lot. The purple key can be found by cutting the grass, and this grass can also be given to your ally to stun Dessa.

HELLO
my name is
Dessa

How can I help you today?
URT

The Store is spread over two levels, and entered via the underground garage. It has several departments including gardening supplies, a travel agency, and a café. There's also a loading bay.

After the officer successfully returns with the batteries, The Safe Place picks up a radio signal from another group, located at somewhere called Settlement Six. They agree to meet this group at the Old Oak—where they discover it's led by Willow. One member of The Safe Place used to be part of her gang and has told the others she's bad news. Meanwhile Willow bears a grudge against the officer for arresting her, and kidnaps one of The Safe Place group, Zizzy. The officer follows . . .

CHAPTER 3—REFINERY

ANTAGONIST: Tigry, Baren, Felix, Filip, Kolie, Kitty, Pandy

NOTES: 11

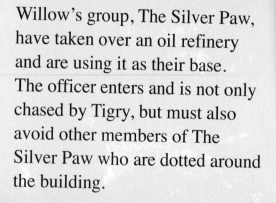

Willow's group, The Silver Paw, have taken over an oil refinery and are using it as their base. The officer enters and is not only chased by Tigry, but must also avoid other members of The Silver Paw who are dotted around the building.

ATTENTION

- Please keep the kitchen clean.

- Wash up after yourself.

- Infections can spread on dirty surfaces!

The Refinery is an industrial building spread over two levels and includes a cafeteria, a kitchen, meeting rooms, and an outside area. Because The Silver Paw have been living here, this location contains a huge number of notes written by them, containing clues as to what's been going on here.

There are Infected here, too, and when the officer finds Zizzy, she's battling one of them, Poley. However, she then notices a scratch—which means she's infected, too, and will soon change. The officer leaves her there and returns to The Safe Place.

TIPS

The secondary antagonists of this chapter are guarding different rooms that you'll need to enter to complete the map. But you shouldn't need to change your strategy too much—keep moving and you should be able to avoid them. You may find the gun particularly useful.

CHAPTER 4—THE SAFE PLACE

ANTAGONIST: Raze

NOTES: 14

An explosion rocks The Safe Place, jolting the officer awake. The Silver Paw have tracked them down and are fighting back—everyone needs to get out. The officer must also rescue three friends along the way—but Raze is chasing them.

TIPS

Once you locate Mimi and Giraffy, they function as allies for the rest of the chapter. You need the blowtorch from the purple safe to open the blowtorch door—this is a new element introduced into the game for this chapter. The elevator key is also a new element.

WARNING!

Do not use this blowtorch without appropriate safety protection. Wear the goggles and gloves provided.

(Unless you're trying to escape from someone and are in a really big hurry.)

This is one of the largest maps in the game, with six levels. Rooms here include six bedrooms, a radio room, a laundry room, a gymnasium, and various corridors and storage rooms. There are fourteen notes to find, too!

Unfortunately after all that effort spent escaping the building, the officer runs straight into Willow and her loyal minions. Willow's angry—the raid on the Refinery meant they had to relocate everyone who was living there. The officer and other Safe Place members are taken to one of Willow's other outposts, the Factory, and locked in a cell.

CHAPTER 5—SEWERS

ANTAGONIST: Alfis

NOTES: 7

A way out of the cell at the Factory presents itself—there's a sewer cover inside the cell, and members of The Safe Place group have made their way through the Sewers and opened the cover. They need help opening a cell door. The officer leaves with them, telling the others to stay here for now to avoid attracting suspicion.

CROCODILES IN SEWERS "A MYTH" SAY EXPERTS

There is no truth in stories of a civilization of crocodiles living in the sewers underneath Lucella, say experts familiar with the sewer system.

"There's just no evidence for it," says Dr. Polly of Lucella University. "Crocodiles want to live in comfortable homes like the rest of us. They've got no reason to lurk in sewers."

The Sewers are spread over two levels, with rooms leading off, including storage rooms and engine rooms. It's another large map, with a fairly chaotic layout.

Once the cell door is open, you're found by one of Willow's associates—who decides not to stop you, as he's been ill-treated by The Silver Paw. Willow shoots at the escapees, but Giraffy takes the bullet. The others take Giraffy away in the hope of saving him while the officer confronts Willow . . .

TIPS

This chapter introduces a different type of antagonist. Alfis is faster than the usual NPC antagonist, and rather than just chasing the player, he lays Default Traps around the map. Listen for his soundtrack and you'll know if he's chasing you. Two gears are needed to get the machine working and drain the water.

CHAPTER 6—FACTORY

ANTAGONISTS: Kolie and Willow

NOTES: 7

Willow remarks that it sounds like something's coming up from the Sewers. She also says it doesn't seem very fair that she's got a weapon, so she gives the officer a head start to escape through the Factory. She shoots out a light . . .

As the officer dashes through the Factory, looking for something to fight back with, they may find six members of

TIPS

Kolie and Willow can both place Default Traps, and Willow also has her revolver, which she can use to stun you if you get too near. Note that saving every Silver Paw member requires a different tool, so getting them all isn't a quick job!

SILVER PAW CHORES

BAREN—move boxes out of room

PANDY—paint wall

Need a volunteer to fix the broken fence

The Silver Paw—who, as it happens, are all in dangerous situations. One is stuck in a room that's on fire, another has become trapped under a pile of boxes, and so on. The officer can choose to save them—or leave them there . . .

This is the first chapter to branch off into different versions of the story. Saving all six members of The Silver Paw leads to the Savior Ending, while getting just some of them leads to the Survivor Ending. In both of these, Willow tries to shoot the officer but is convinced not to by Kolie: The difference is that anyone you failed to save will not be present. If you don't save anyone, Willow shoots you and the screen turns to black (though the story will still continue).

CHAPTER 7—PORT

ANTAGONIST: Dakoda

NOTES: 6

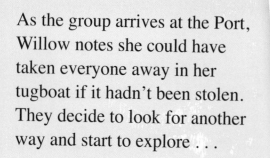

As the group arrives at the Port, Willow notes she could have taken everyone away in her tugboat if it hadn't been stolen. They decide to look for another way and start to explore . . .

There are several different buildings in Port, including two that are accessible and both have four stories. Most important

DO NOT
COME INTO
PORT

Danger of infection
Save yourselves!

there's a lighthouse, which is the ultimate target of the chapter (if you're on the Savior narrative path, Mimi will have pointed this out at the start).

Once the lighthouse is working, a ship called the *Medora*, steered by Captain Budgey, comes into Port. The group ask Budgey for help, but Budgey says it's impossible— she used what little fuel she had to bring the ship in. She does have spare fuel, but it's sealed in the hold along with infected members of the *Medora*'s crew. Willow offers to go down there and get it—and the officer volunteers to go, too . . .

TIPS

If you find and click all five Eyes of Insolence around the Port, then knock on the locked door of the building on the far right, you'll release a hidden antagonist that is very fast and will swiftly kill you. There's no reward for doing so, though!

CHAPTER 8—SHIP

ANTAGONISTS: Archie, Bobby, Kenneth, Pepper

NOTES: 10

Captain Budgey tells the officer and Willow that the fuel is in the hull of the ship. The *Medora*, it turns out, is a pretty big ship, with six levels, so getting there isn't easy. Rooms include a radio room, a control room, a cargo room, a cafeteria, a bunk room and an engine room.

TIPS

To solve the color-code puzzle, you need to look on the screens in the bridge. In addition to the usual notes, further lore clues can be found by listening to the radio: There's a coded message and a backward one.

CREW MANIFEST

CAPTAIN BUDGEY
PEPPER
ARCHIE
KENNETH
BOBBY

The officer and Willow locate the crate containing the fuel, finding just enough to get them across the sea . . . but they're shoved inside it by Kenneth. Willow isn't happy to be trapped in a crate with a "dirty cop," and despite the officer's protests that they were just doing their job, Willow demands to know where her parents are—she hasn't seen them since their arrest over a decade ago. The officer doesn't know what happened to them.

Fortunately the other members of the group find and release the officer and Willow, and the *Medora* is able to continue on its way. There are flashes in the sky as the ship arrives at its destination . . .

CHAPTER 9—DOCKS

ANTAGONISTS: Markus, Crawling Trap

NOTES: 7

The *Medora* has arrived in Doveport, and Captain Budgey bids farewell to his passengers while Willow spots Tigry in the distance. The officer seeks a safe route to the surface.

The Docks consist of a number of rooms below ground level, with several dock spaces for boat maintenance. But there's

Dear Sir,
We at the Archaeological Society are still awaiting your reply to our request for permission to conduct a survey at your docks, as we believe there may be a site of great historical interest there.

Yours in anticipation,

DECLINED

also a hidden tomb—one of the notes says, "Do you think they had any idea a tomb was here when they built the Docks?"

At the end the officer meets Tigry, who apologizes for trying to hunt them down. When the officer says they're searching for a cure, Tigry

warns against trusting Willow and says he'll help if they ditch her. The officer declines—and the group moves on. Walking across a snowy landscape, they meet Kona, inventor of the mall security droid, who's now studying the Infected.

TIPS

Dynamite makes its first appearance in Book 2, and there's also a new mechanic in the form of the candle. The solution to the Roman numeral code is on the wall of the tomb, inside the brick labyrinth, and at the end of the walkway near the plank gap. If you can escape this map without Pony being attacked, you can start on the path toward a hidden ending . . .

CHAPTER 10—TEMPLE

ANTAGONIST: Spidella

NOTES: 8

Kona allows the group to escape through his lab and sends his robot Robby with them for protection. They emerge into the Temple, a building located on a snowy mountainside, with a high-tech area and a bridge across a chasm, where they are menaced by Spidella. They escape the Temple . . .

TIPS

This chapter has a shape code that must be solved to unlock the door. Two parts of the solution can be found in the green and blue key rooms (which are also the possible spawn points for the candle), while the other is just along the passage from the shovel obstruction. Note that the arrow on each clue shows where the center of the wheel would be.

DAY 43
Need more test subjects . . .
Where's an Infected when you
need one? I see a ship coming
in . . . Maybe they have some . . .

DAY 44
No luck—all uninfected. They seem
like a nice enough bunch . . .
Maybe they'll find a cure? Then
what will I do with my time?

In the Survivor narrative, they reach the surface and Robby volunteers to stay and look after the children while the officer, Willow, and Pony carry on.

But in the Savior narrative, the officer feels odd and has a vision of a strange figure who says he became curious about the officer due to them having avoided infection for so long. The figure tells the officer they're uniquely immune to the Infection, and offers help, which the officer declines. The figure tells the officer to "stay out of my business. If you continue to follow your current path, you will live to regret it."

CHAPTER 11—CAMP

ANTAGONISTS: Delta, Ben, Eloise, Mary, Porter

NOTES: 5

The group arrives at a military Camp in Blizzard Vale: in the Savior narrative, Kona guides Mimi over the walkie-talkie, warning the group to be careful. The officer notes the lack of damage, suggesting the Infected took them by surprise and there wasn't much of a fight.

WATCHTOWER LOG

11:00: Nothing to report.

00:00: All quiet.

01:00: Still quiet.

02:00: Nothing happening.

03:00: Noises in distance?

04:00: HELP ME I'M TRAPPED AT THE TOP OF THIS WATCHTOWER!

The Camp includes two watchtowers, a cave, a medical base, and some offices. Delta roams the Camp and attacks when anyone comes near. Four secondary antagonists—all Soldiers in uniform—can be tackled by allies.

After the Camp is cleared, in the Savior narrative, certain shocking facts come to light:

Way back in the Forest in Book 1, it was Pony who dosed Doggy with Substance 128, on the instructions of Willow. He also gave Substance 128 to the officer and was surprised they weren't infected. The officer is willing to forgive, and after an encounter with Tigry, they move on . . .

TIPS

This chapter has a light code by the final door, with the parts of the code located in the cabin with the Howitzer on top, in the unlocked cabin on the upper level with all the screens (look between the lockers), and behind the green key cabin, also on the upper level.

HEIST

A flashback returns us to the Alleys, back before Willow's arrest. Willow's younger brother, William, is upset and won't even talk to her. Billy has a great idea: They can't buy him anything, because they're broke—but they can steal something nice for him. They'll go to the Baba's Pies warehouse and steal a pie for William.

TIPS

This chapter randomly assigns you to play as Willow or Pony, but gameplay isn't affected by this. The mechanics are fairly simple, though an item unique to this chapter is the spray can, which is used to reveal the lasers. As with other character-POV chapters, Heist was made a VIP exclusive after its initial release.

IDEAS OF NICE THINGS TO STEAL FOR WILLIAM
- Lollipop
- Dinosaur (toy, not real)
- Traffic cone
- Ukulele
- Fancy hat
- Fish that sings when you clap your hands
- PIE ✓

Unfortunately Officer Poley discovers their plan and chases them around the Alleys, trying to stop them. Compared to the Alleys map, more of the area is visible. When Willow finally gets the pie, she returns home with it—only to find William has gone. His scarf is lying on the floor . . .

Soon after this, Willow was arrested (as seen in Chapter 1)—but while she was in a cell, Poley became infected and dropped the key. Willow also visited Rash, who was also infected: She locked him in a room above a laundromat. And then she formed The Silver Paw, and sought revenge on the police who arrested her—and her parents. But she still doesn't know what happened to William, even now . . .

DISTRACTION

NOTES: 3

Another character-focused chapter, this time telling the story of what happened to Zizzy after she was released from her cell at the Refinery. She's been scratched and knows the Infection will set in before long. She needs to cause a distraction to aid the escape of her friends . . .

IMPORTANT

In the event of an explosion, please move toward the exits in an orderly fashion. Do not stop to collect any belongings. They may explode, too.

Due to the Infection taking hold, the Refinery appears distorted compared to when it was last seen—and Zizzy is being pursued by her own twin sisters, who seem to be infected themselves. (As this never actually happened, it seems this is a hallucination.) The best way to create a distraction is to find some dynamite and blow up the entire Refinery . . .

After she escapes, Zizzy runs into the same mysterious figure encountered by the officer. He admires her strength and resilience, and asks her to join him. He tells her that when he was young, "I felt alone often, so I made myself a friend. One from beyond." She's about to accept his offer, but then an arm drags her into a portal . . .

TIPS

The dynamite is located on a shelf in the room opened by the green key, on a bench inside the maze, and in the kitchen.

CHAPTER 12—LAB

ANTAGONIST: Distorted Piggy, The Iniquitous One, Crawling Trap, Sentinels

NOTES: 6

Inside the cave at the Camp is a Lab—which is where the cure is located. All the officer has to do is find it. The Lab is a high-tech facility on two floors, with a series of code switches. While opening up the Lab and trying not to get killed, the officer experiences a whiteout . . .

And then finds themselves in a distorted world where elements of previous chapters are mashed together. Willow and Tigry stand ready to fight in an arena. Three weapons can be found scattered around the map: a water gun, a mop, and a pipe. The officer can choose to give these weapons to either of the two fighters . . .

THE END?

The outcome depends on whether you're following the Savior or the Survivor narrative, and whether you helped Willow or Tigry win their fight. There are endings where you are forced to join with The Iniquitous One to save your friends. There are endings where you do find the cure but end up not giving it to a friend who betrayed you. There's also a Hidden Ending, in which the cure is found—but The Iniquitous One warns it will start a fresh war. The officer disagrees and, after realizing The Iniquitous One has trapped them inside their own memories, uses this against them to defeat them in battle. There is hope for the future after all . . .

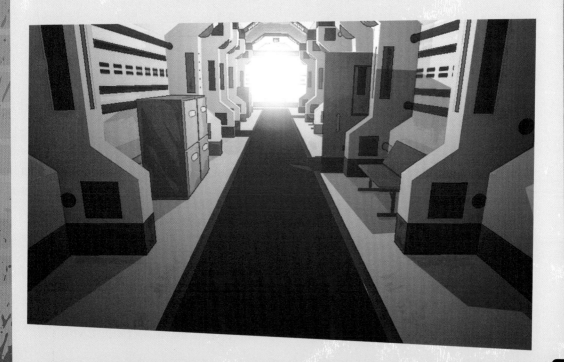

BREAKOUT

ANTAGONISTS: Ombra, The Hand

NOTES: 13

A bonus character-POV chapter filling in some of Tigry's backstory in his military days. He's in a trench with his comrade Danny, being commanded by Sergeant Monroe to capture an enemy bunker. As he dashes toward the bunker, dodging explosions, the ground collapses and he falls into a lower level of the bunker.

TIPS

To unlock the color-code pads, you need to consult the whiteboard in the conference room. There's a map of the bunker with three of the color pad locations marked with the color you need to press. The final pad won't have its color marked, but it'll be the color that the other three don't use. You can just guess these, but the pad will lock for a few seconds after each wrong guess.

Congratulations, Soldier!
You've passed your training with flying colors. Your first taste of combat isn't far away.

Finding himself in the dark with no weapons, Tigry looks for a way to get the power on—but he's pursued by Ombra, a terrifying distorted tigerlike creature. Eventually he finds a knife and manages to stab Ombra . . .

Further flashbacks reveal Tigry was bullied at school and neglected at home, which led to him running away and joining the army. After proving his worth, he was sent to fight . . . at which point, it becomes clear Ombra was a hallucination, and he actually stabbed Danny. After leaving the military, while wandering lost and dejected, he meets Willow . . .

WINTER HOLIDAY

This chapter was originally released after Chapter 4 of Book 2, but it doesn't occur there in the timeline: It's a Christmas special rather than part of the main story and was removed from the game after being live for just over a month. It's since been made live again for the holiday season.

Dear Santa,
This year, please bring me the antidote for Substance 128.
I promise I have been very good.

In it, The Safe Place gang are vacationing at a cabin when the officer realizes they don't have presents for everyone. The officer says they'll be right back and dashes off to look for presents—while being pursued by the mysterious Frostiggy. The map contains other cabins, an ice fort, and a hedge maze.

Once all the presents are safely retrieved, the officer mentions to the others that they were being chased the whole time by Frostiggy . . . but somehow none of the others saw it. It's all forgotten as they're delighted by their gifts and thank the officer.

TIPS

There are five presents to find: a book, a dreidel, a carrot, a fencing foil, and a robot toy, all of which must be brought back to the Christmas tree to trigger the ending. The Frostiggy skin is a reward for completing the chapter.

WILLOW

FIRST STORY APPEARANCE: Book 2, Chapter 1
SKIN INTRODUCED: Book 2, Chapter 12
OBTAINABLE: Complete Player's Journal
WEAPON: Revolver

Willow has a huge role in Book 2, and along the way, it's revealed she was behind some of the events of Book 1. Before the Infection, she and her brother, William, were placed in foster care after their parents were arrested. However, their foster mother, Daisy, was called up to military service, leaving Willow and William to fend for themselves. They had to steal food to survive.

Willow has since formed the survivors' group The Silver Paw and wants revenge on Doggy and the player for arresting her back then. She's one of two possible viewpoint characters in the Heist chapter.

OFFICER DOGGY

FIRST STORY APPEARANCE: Book 2, Chapter 1
SKIN INTRODUCED: Book 2, Chapter 1
OBTAINABLE: 275 Tokens
WEAPON: Taser

Of course, we've met Doggy before, early in Book 1, but the flashback that forms the first chapter of Book 2 sees him at an earlier time, wearing his police uniform. As that takes place before the Infection, the NPC version of Officer Doggy is not infected, though the skin you can acquire does have infected eyes.

During the Alley's incident, we see Doggy's black-and-white view of law enforcement. Even though Willow was forced into stealing food for her own survival, Doggy refuses to bend the rules for her and arrests her anyway—which leads to Willow bearing a grudge against him.

 RASH

FIRST STORY APPEARANCE: Book 2, Chapter 1
SKIN INTRODUCED: Book 2, Chapter 1
OBTAINABLE: 300 Tokens
WEAPON: Crowbar

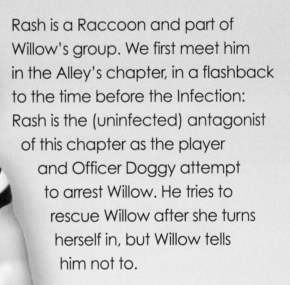

Rash is a Raccoon and part of Willow's group. We first meet him in the Alley's chapter, in a flashback to the time before the Infection: Rash is the (uninfected) antagonist of this chapter as the player and Officer Doggy attempt to arrest Willow. He tries to rescue Willow after she turns herself in, but Willow tells him not to.

Rash is seen again from a different perspective in Heist, where the player is a member of Willow's gang. This time Rash is an ally. Later we learn he became infected and Willow was forced to lock him in a room.

PANDY

FIRST STORY APPEARANCE: Book 2, Chapter 2
SKIN INTRODUCED: Book 1, Chapter 5
OBTAINABLE: 160 Tokens/350 Tokens
WEAPON: Bamboo Stick/Katana

Pandy was introduced to the game as a skin in Book 1, but she didn't appear in the story until Book 2, along with a whole different version of her skin, which carries a katana instead of a bamboo stick. She is a member of the group of survivors known as The Silver Paw.

When Pandy makes her first story appearance in Chapter 2, Store, she is an antagonist and continues to be one in Chapter 3, Refinery. She later becomes an ally in Chapter 6, Factory, where the player has the option to save her after she becomes trapped on a high platform.

🐻 DESSA

FIRST STORY APPEARANCE: Book 2, Chapter 2
SKIN INTRODUCED: Book 2, Chapter 2
OBTAINABLE: 375 Tokens
WEAPON: Bo Staff/Candy Cane

Dessa is the antagonist of Chapter 2, Store. The end credits of Book 2 confirm that, prior to the Infection, she was a cashier at the store. A tweet by the creator of *PIGGY*, MiniToon, in 2021 confirmed Dessa is a transgender woman.

Dessa's weapon, the bo staff, appears in the game catalog under that name. (Do they sell those at the store, or did she bring it in herself?) There's also a Christmas variant of Dessa called Reindessa, who costs the same but has a holiday-themed outfit and weapon.

🐻 BAREN

FIRST STORY APPEARANCE: Book 2, Chapter 2
SKIN INTRODUCED: N/A
OBTAINABLE: N/A
WEAPON: Axe

Baren is a bear, and one of the most significant characters not to be made available as a skin. He's a member of Willow's group The Silver Paw, making his first appearance during events at the Store, and in the Refinery chapter he's a secondary antagonist.

Baren is one of The Silver Paw members you can rescue during the crucial events of Chapter 6, at the Factory: A pile of boxes have fallen on him, and you can release him from this fate. After this he becomes friendly.

🐻 RAZE

FIRST STORY APPEARANCE: Book 2, Chapter 4
SKIN INTRODUCED: Book 2, Chapter 4
OBTAINABLE: 400 Tokens
WEAPON: Drill Arms

Raze is a Rat and also a cyborg—as indicated by his drill arms and his ear being replaced by a gear. After an explosion in the area of The Safe Place, Raze appears and pursues the inhabitants of The Safe Place.

How Raze became a cyborg hasn't been explained—it may have been before he was infected, or afterward. (Cyborg technology is clearly in use in this world, as seen in other characters.) Barbed wire is wrapped around the top of his drills.

ALFIS

FIRST STORY APPEARANCE: Book 2, Chapter 5
SKIN INTRODUCED: Book 2, Chapter 5
OBTAINABLE: 450 Tokens
WEAPON: Rusty Pipe

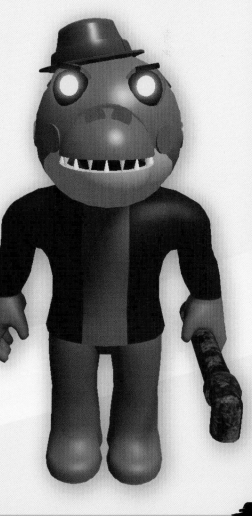

If you thought alligators lurking in sewers were just an urban myth, think again! Chapter 5 takes place in the Sewers, and Alfis is the main antagonist. His outfit, which includes a brown fedora, was inspired by Indiana Jones.

Alfis is the first NPC in the game to have the orange eyes that suggest he's a member of the Insolence, a group under the influence of the Eye. He's also the first of a smarter breed of *PIGGY* bot, as he searches for the player and places traps for you.

 # MARI

FIRST STORY APPEARANCE: N/A
SKIN INTRODUCED: Book 2, Chapter 5
OBTAINABLE: 500 Tokens
WEAPON: None

Mari is the first Book 2 skin not to feature anywhere in the story. While most of the *PIGGY* characters are living animals, Mari is a toy animal: A marionette of a mouse, and not one in great condition, either, as one of its infected eyes is popping out of its socket.

Those infected eyes are orange, suggesting it might be part of the Insolence: Maybe the Eye has power over things that were never alive? Another unusual aspect is that Mari doesn't carry a weapon or have one as part of its body: It kills you with its bare hands . . .

🐨 KOLIE

FIRST STORY APPEARANCE: Book 2, Chapter 6
SKIN INTRODUCED: Book 2, Chapter 6
OBTAINABLE: 425 Tokens
WEAPON: Maces

Kolie is a Koala and worker at the factory. The right-hand side of his face is entirely black, which could be the result of an accident—but his orange eye indicates an association with the Insolence, and he's not the only one with an orange eye and a blackened face.

Kolie's weapons can be found in the game catalog, where they are listed as the Spikey Stick of Civilized Negotiation. He makes a further, brief appearance in the Hidden Ending that can be unlocked at Chapter 12.

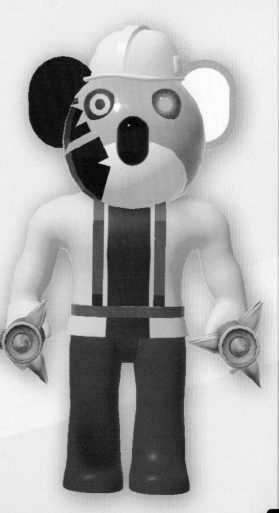

 # DAISY

FIRST STORY APPEARANCE: Book 2, Chapter 6
SKIN INTRODUCED: Book 1, Distorted Memory
OBTAINABLE: 245 Tokens
WEAPON: Plank with Nail

Daisy is a Donkey. The origin of her weapon is that she tried to build a fence to keep out the Infected. When it was broken down, she used part of it to attack others.

Daisy has a role in the story of Book 2, though she isn't an antagonist or ally. She owns a shop called Daisy's TVs, which can be found in Chapter 1, Alleys, but she first appears in flashback at the end of Chapter 6. She became foster mother to Willow and William but had to leave them behind after being called up to the military. While at the military camp in Doveport, she became infected—as seen at the end of Heist.

 BUDGEY

FIRST STORY APPEARANCE: Book 2, Chapter 7
SKIN INTRODUCED: 2020 Custom Skin Contest
OBTAINABLE: 525 Tokens
WEAPON: Hook

The winner of the 2020 Custom Skin Contest was another pirate-themed design, created by Midnight. Budgey is a pirate budgerigar—the first bird to appear in *PIGGY*—with a hook at the end of her left wing instead of a talon.

Budgey was later added to the story, and she features in Book 2, at the Port. The crew of her ship, the *Medora*, have all been infected, leaving her as the last survivor. She agrees to take the player's group across the sea before leaving the story line in Chapter 9, Docks.

 DAKODA

FIRST STORY APPEARANCE: Book 2, Chapter 7
SKIN INTRODUCED: Book 2, Chapter 7
OBTAINABLE: 460 Tokens
WEAPON: Anchor

It's hard to tell what type of animal Dakoda is under all that diving gear, but they're actually a Dugong, a marine mammal related to the manatee. They are the main antagonist at the Port.

Their diving suit is the old-fashioned type with a metallic spherical helmet with a grille window in the front: This style of helmet is called a bathysphere and it can be found in the game catalog under that name. (The anchor, however, is different from the one in the catalog.)

KRAXICORDE

FIRST STORY APPEARANCE: N/A
SKIN INTRODUCED: Book 2, Chapter 7
OBTAINABLE: 700 Tokens
WEAPON: Tentacles

Kraxicorde is a Kraken, the legendary sea monster of Norwegian mythology that could wrap itself around ships and pull them beneath the waves. He has four legs and three eyes (an earlier design just had two eyes).

Although Kraxicorde was introduced alongside a highly appropriate chapter in the form of Port (and there was an idea he might be larger than the *Medora*), he doesn't feature in the chapter itself, and only appears as a skin. He glows in the dark—though the effect doesn't fully work on mobile devices.

 ARCHIE

FIRST STORY APPEARANCE: Book 2, Chapter 8
SKIN INTRODUCED: Book 2, Chapter 8
OBTAINABLE: 385 Tokens
WEAPON: Fire Extinguisher

Archie is an Arctic Fox, and he was a member of Captain Budgey's crew, who became infected, aboard the *Medora*. At some point, either during or after his infection, Archie suffered a horrific injury, resulting in his skull being exposed on the right-hand side of his head.

Archie is the main antagonist of Chapter 8. Captain Budgey sealed him in the hold of the *Medora* for her own safety—however, this also sealed her off from the ship's fuel, meaning the officer and Willow have to get past him when they go to fetch it.

🐷 KAMOSI

FIRST STORY APPEARANCE: N/A
SKIN INTRODUCED: Book 2, Chapter 8
OBTAINABLE: 550 Tokens
WEAPON: Claws

Following on from Skelly and Zompiggy, here's another *PIGGY* version of a popular monster. Kamosi is an Egyptian-style mummy and has a similar name to the Egyptian pharaoh Kamose, who was mummified after his death.

Kamosi was released with Chapter 8, Ship, and though they don't appear in the level itself, it's an apt choice, as many Egyptian mummies were taken from their burial places, after being unearthed by archaeologists, and shipped to other countries. You wouldn't want to be trapped on board with one of these if it woke up . . .

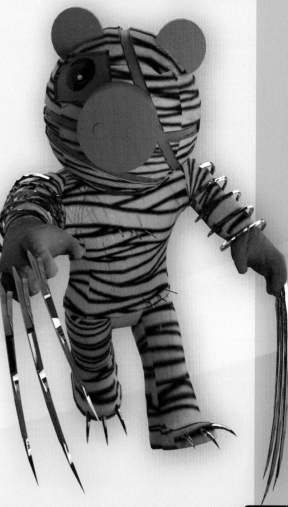

 MARKUS

FIRST STORY APPEARANCE: Book 2, Chapter 9
SKIN INTRODUCED: Book 2, Chapter 9
OBTAINABLE: 425 Tokens
WEAPON: Pitchfork

Markus is a Moose and farmer, who is the main antagonist at the Docks. His antlers can impede him when moving around the map—but he can teleport, the first *PIGGY* character with this ability. His pitchfork can be found in the game catalog under the name Farmer's Revenge.

Some clue to Markus's background may be found in a note, located at the Docks, in which the note's author says he's "just a farmer who wanted an adventure" but encountered "Dark creatures . . . everywhere." It seems likely Markus is the farmer who came to the Docks for an adventure.

KONA

FIRST STORY APPEARANCE: Book 2, Chapter 9
SKIN INTRODUCED: Book 2, Chapter 9
OBTAINABLE: 335 Tokens
WEAPON: Blowtorch

Kona is a Klipspringer (a type of antelope) and an engineer: He's the one who created Robby. The Robby prototype was his assistant before the Infection, and he was strongly against the "upgrades" that installed Chainsaw Arms onto his creations.

Kona is an eccentric character, and when he enters the story, he's conducting research into the Infected. When Doveport was evacuated, he stayed behind, unwilling to be separated from his research. He meets The Safe Place group and allows them to leave through the route in his lab.

PHENNA

FIRST STORY APPEARANCE: N/A
SKIN INTRODUCED: Book 2, Chapter 10
OBTAINABLE: Quest Completion
WEAPON: Spikes

Phenna is a Phoenix who can only be obtained by completing a quest in the Temple chapter. You need the candle for this. Enter a room with a swinging axe and use the candle to light the question mark on the wall: It should change, activating the quest.

Go around the map looking for more question marks to activate, and then look for the symbol near each one. These can spawn in different places. Write down or remember each symbol. Then go to an upstairs brick room with these symbols on the wall. Press the symbols in the sequence you found them.

SPIDELLA

FIRST STORY APPEARANCE: Book 2, Chapter 10
SKIN INTRODUCED: Book 2, Chapter 10
OBTAINABLE: 625 Tokens
WEAPON: Spikes

Spidella is a Spider, dressed in a very elegant black coat. She is the antagonist at the Temple, and the only one in the game to use Slow Traps. (All other trap-using NPCs use Default Traps, except for Delta.)

Spidella is one of the smallest characters in the game, but her skin is one of the most expensive to buy. She also has one of the most interesting jumpscares, striking the victim in two different ways—she first lashes out with her back spikes, then follows it up with a punch.

 DELTA

FIRST STORY APPEARANCE: Book 2, Chapter 11
SKIN INTRODUCED: Book 2, Chapter 11
OBTAINABLE: 485 Tokens
WEAPON: Bazooka

We don't know what type of animal Delta is under that face mask and those goggles—but we do know he's a Soldier. All this makes him a lot like Torcher from Book 1. His name has echoes of Delta Force, a special unit of the US Army primarily involved in counterterrorism.

Judging from his orange eye, he seems to be one of the Insolence. He's the main antagonist in the Camp in Chapter 11, and he has the ability to place Big Traps around the map.

🐻 LAURA

FIRST STORY APPEARANCE: N/A
SKIN INTRODUCED: Book 2, Chapter 11
OBTAINABLE: Quest Completion
WEAPON: Teddy Bear

Laura is a Lemur who can only be obtained by completing a quest in the Camp chapter of Book 2. First you need to complete enough of the map to reach the exit elevator inside the cave. Look on the side of the elevator and you will see an Insolence eye, which you can click to start the quest.

You now need to collect all six parts of Laura's teddy bear, which spawn at various locations around the map. Once you have them all, go to the blue cabin with all the screens in it. The teddy bear should be under one of the screens. Lure a Soldier into the cabin and over to the teddy bear to complete the quest.

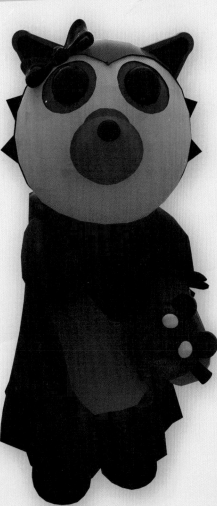

🐷 BILLY

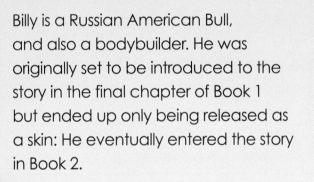

FIRST STORY APPEARANCE: Book 2, Heist
SKIN INTRODUCED: Book 1, Chapter 12
OBTAINABLE: 500 Tokens
WEAPON: Barbell

Billy is a Russian American Bull, and also a bodybuilder. He was originally set to be introduced to the story in the final chapter of Book 1 but ended up only being released as a skin: He eventually entered the story in Book 2.

He is a friend of Willow, and in the Heist chapter we see the heist was originally his idea: The group wanted to give William something nice to cheer him up, but as they had no money, Billy suggested stealing something. The target of this heist was a pie.

🐷 TOBI

FIRST STORY APPEARANCE: N/A
SKIN INTRODUCED: Book 2, Heist
OBTAINABLE: 465 Tokens
WEAPON: Fire Hose

Although Tobi was added as a skin along with the Heist chapter, he doesn't feature in that chapter, or anywhere else in the game. He's a Tortoise, though he lacks a shell—and to be fair, if he had a shell he wouldn't be able to get his firefighter's jacket on.

Tobi's infected pupil is yellow, and the pupil colors of members of the Infected are significant, reflecting what they did in their former life. A yellow pupil indicates someone who served their community—which makes sense, with Tobi being a firefighter.

🐷 SENTINEL

FIRST STORY APPEARANCE: Book 2, Distraction
SKIN INTRODUCED: Book 1, Chapter 12
OBTAINABLE: Collect All Pages
WEAPON: None

Sentinel, a dark, monstrous Pig with eyes, ribs, and fingers that glow different colors, was introduced as a skin at the end of Book 1, unlocked if the player collects all the pages.

However, it later made a story appearance in Book 2: An array of different-colored Sentinels are the secondary antagonists in Distraction. These can be killed with a pipe. The Sentinels also pop up in Chapter 12. They appear to serve the Insolence, but what they actually *are* is never revealed.

⬤ SILZOUS

FIRST STORY APPEARANCE: N/A
SKIN INTRODUCED: Book 2, Chapter 12
OBTAINABLE: 725 Tokens
WEAPON: Axe

Silzous holds the honor of being *PIGGY*'s most expensive skin, at a huge cost of 725 Piggy Tokens. He's a Snake with horns who carries an enormous axe, and his creator, TenuousFlea, has confirmed he's a member of the Insolence.

The soundtrack that plays when Silzous gets a kill, "Sinful Snake," has an unusual feature—lyrics! "My dark influence shall rise one day, in a hideous way. No one shall stay awake, I'm a sinful snake." He originally had a second song, "Flaming Desert," that was removed for technical reasons.

 OMBRA

FIRST STORY APPEARANCE: Book 2, Breakout
SKIN INTRODUCED: Book 2, Breakout
OBTAINABLE: Complete Chapter
WEAPON: Claws

Ombra is a sort of monstrous, distorted Tiger with two extra, spiderlike arms growing from its back. It has a black body and interior that glows in different colors, similar to the Sentinels—suggesting that it was created by The Iniquitous One.

It appears as the main antagonist of Breakout and is probably a hallucination suffered during the events of that chapter. If you complete the chapter, you receive the skin as a reward. Note that the red and purple Ombras are faster and smaller than the standard one.

118

THE INIQUITOUS ONE

FIRST STORY APPEARANCE: Book 2, Chapter 10
SKIN INTRODUCED: Book 2, Chapter 12
OBTAINABLE: Quest Completion
WEAPON: Claws

This one goes by many names:
The Entity, The Insolent, The Iniquitous
One . . . The main thing is he's
the villain behind this whole story.
As a child he felt alone, and so he
made a friend . . . from beyond.
When they fell out, he was banished
to another dimension. He reaches
people through their subconscious
minds, seeking to recruit them to
serve his own, mysterious ends.

Much of the Iniquitous
One's past and intentions
will probably never be known.
He's ultimately defeated by
turning his manipulation of
others' memories against him.

QUIZ

1) How many stories does House have?

2) What can you give Doggy to make him stun the enemy?

3) Where do you escape into from the School?

4) Where does Mousy hide in Mall?

5) What map is Distorted Memory based on?

6) What are the three endings of Book 1?

7) What was Substance 128 supposed to cure?

8) What sort of animal is Teacher?

9) Which gamemode was introduced at the same time as Devil?

10) What chapter was Parasee originally designed for?

11) In Book 2, what's the reason for visiting the Store?

12) What's the name of Willow's survivor group?

13) What are the two story paths you can follow from Chapter 6 of Book 2?

14) What is Captain Budgey's ship called?

15) In Heist, what does Willow's gang decide to steal for William?

16) What's the name of Dessa's Christmas variant?

17) What's the most expensive skin in Piggy?

18) What are two other names for the Iniquitous One?

19) Poley was released as a crossover with which game?

20) Some limited-time skins like Bakari, Anteo, and Gryffyn can be obtained by collecting a particular number of special items. What is that number?

VAULTED!

Many Piggy skins have been introduced for limited-time events and then put in the vault, out of reach of any players who failed to obtain them. Here's a rundown of some of our favorites—are you lucky enough to own any of these?

CROVE

EVENT: Spooky Hunt
OBTAINABLE: 500 Tokens
WEAPON: Scythe

Crove is a crow who wears a black robe with a hood, and carries a scythe like the Grim Reaper. The scythe is unusual as it can be thrown during Crove's jumpscare, like a boomerang. And while you can't get Crove anymore, you can find the scythe in the Roblox catalog.

POLEY

EVENT: Jailbreak Crossover
OBTAINABLE: Quest Completion
WEAPON: Baton

Poley is a polar bear, and also a police officer in the style of Jailbreak, in a skin introduced for a crossover with that game. While it's no longer obtainable in the main game, you can still find it in the 100-player version of Piggy.

MR. STITCHY

EVENT: Spooky Hunt
OBTAINABLE: Quest Completion
WEAPON: None

Mr. Stitchy is a creepy teddy bear and one of the game's taller characters. He could be obtained during Spooky Hunt by carrying out a quest in Forest. He's unusual in that he carries a lantern but doesn't use it as his weapon.

OWELL

EVENT: Spooky Hunt
OBTAINABLE: Quest Completion
WEAPON: Broom

Owell is an owl dressed like a witch, who not only rides her broomstick but uses it as a weapon. She came out in the second update of Spooky Hunt and could be obtained by completing a quest at Store.

PRIMROSE

EVENT: Winter Holiday Hunt
OBTAINABLE: Quest Completion
WEAPON: Bow and Candy Cane

Quite a few limited-time skins are birds. Primrose is a penguin dressed like an elf, who could be obtained by completing a quest at Refinery during the Winter Holiday Hunt. Instead of arrows, she keeps a candy cane inside her quiver and fires it using her bow.

FROSTIGGY

EVENT: Winter Holiday Hunt
OBTAINABLE: Quest Completion
WEAPON: Spiked Ice Bat

The antagonist of the special Winter Holiday chapter was also made available as a skin, obtained simply by completing the chapter. Look out for her if Winter Holiday is made available again—you may still be able to add her to your collection!

BESS

EVENT: Egg Hunt
OBTAINABLE: Quest Completion
WEAPON: Basket

Don't put all your eggs in one basket, in case Bess steals it and attacks you with it. She's a rabbit with a ninja vibe, who could be obtained by collecting twelve Easter eggs scattered across the first six chapters of Book 2.

125

ANTEO

EVENT: Lab Event
OBTAINABLE: 1,050 Vials
WEAPON: None

This giant ant (gi-ant?) was available during a special Lab event that involved completing quests to earn vials, which could then be exchanged for the skin. It has the ability to change color, going between brown, red, and green.

BAKARI

EVENT: Haunting Event
OBTAINABLE: 1,050 Candies
WEAPON: None

This bat skin was obtained in a similar way to Anteo—completing quests to earn candies to buy the skin. He can briefly become invisible—the only skin in the game with this ability—and has the unusual feature of a white cross in his eye.